JOHN THOMPSON'S
EASIEST PIANO COURSE

FIRST JAZZ TUNES

CONTENTS

2 **Bye Bye Blackbird**

4 **Ain't She Sweet**

6 **It's Only a Paper Moon**

8 **Blue Skies**

10 **Satin Doll**

12 **The Glory of Love**

14 **Alexander's Ragtime Band**

16 **Night Train**

ISBN 978-1-4803-5080-9

EXCLUSIVELY DISTRIBUTED BY

WILLIS MUSIC

HAL•LEONARD®
CORPORATION
7777 W. BLUEMOUND RD. P.O. BOX 13819
MILWAUKEE, WISCONSIN 53213

Bye Bye Blackbird

from PETE KELLY'S BLUES

Lyric by Mort Dixon
Music by Ray Henderson
Arranged by Eric Baumgartner

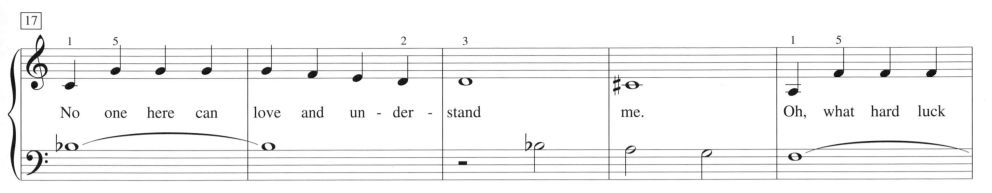

No one here can love and un-der-stand me. Oh, what hard luck

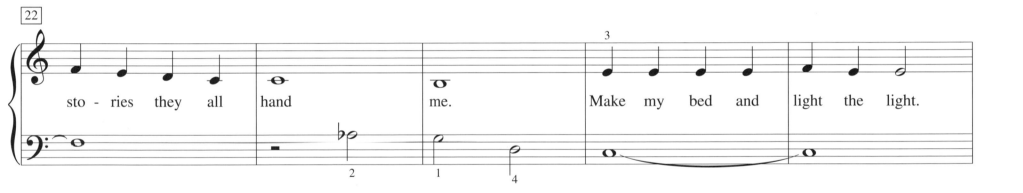

sto-ries they all hand me. Make my bed and light the light.

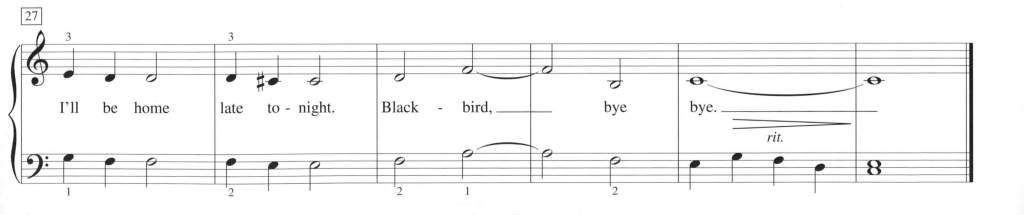

I'll be home late to-night. Black-bird, _____ bye bye. _____

rit.

Ain't She Sweet

Many jazz pieces use eighth notes that are played "unevenly" to give it a cool jazz feel.
These are called *swing eighths*.
The first note of each pair is played slightly longer than
the second. Swing eighths are often indicated by this instruction:

Words by Jack Yellen
Music by Milton Ager
Arranged by Eric Baumgartner

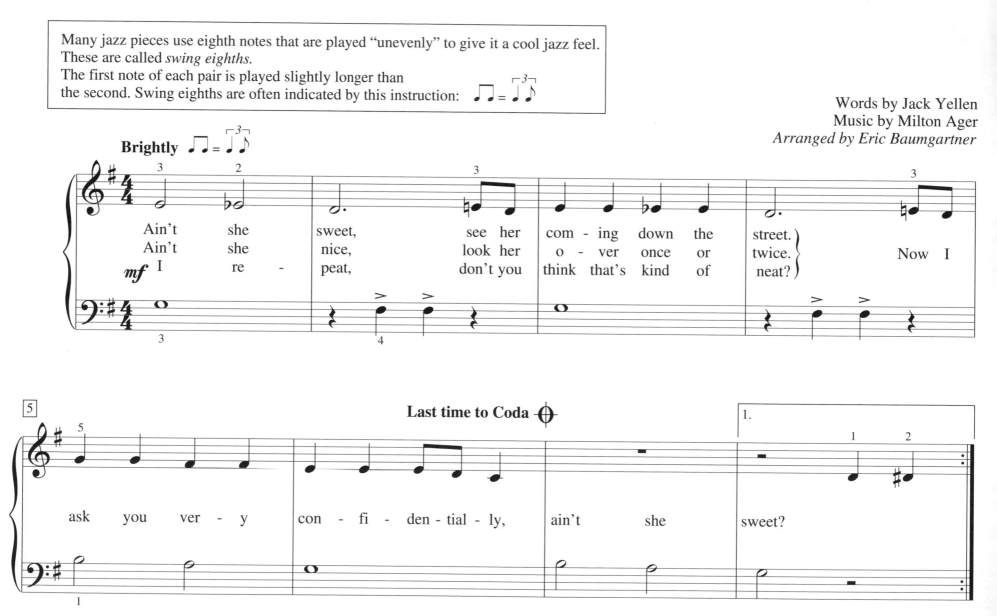

© 1927 WARNER BROS. INC.
© Renewed EDWIN H. MORRIS & COMPANY, A Division of MPL Music Publishing, Inc. and WARNER BROS. INC.
This arrangement © 2013 EDWIN H. MORRIS & COMPANY, A Division of MPL Music Publishing, Inc. and WARNER BROS. INC.

It's Only a Paper Moon

Lyric by Billy Rose and E.Y. "Yip" Harburg
Music by Harold Arlen
Arranged by Eric Baumgartner

Say, it's on-ly a pa-per moon, sail-ing o-ver a
Yes, it's on-ly a can-vas sky, hang-ing o-ver a
It's a Bar-num and Bai-ley world, just as pho-ny as

card-board sea. But it would-n't be make-be-lieve if
mus-lin tree.
it can be.

you be-lieved in me.
me. With-

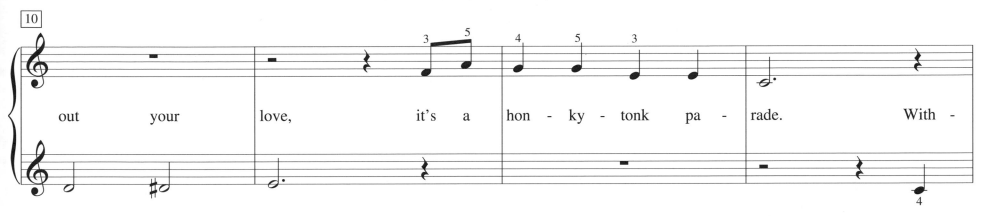

out your love, it's a hon - ky - tonk pa - rade. With -

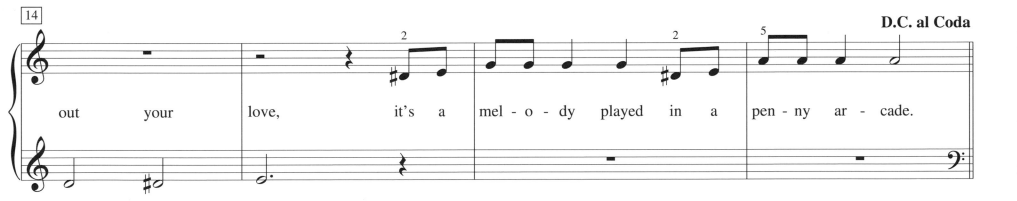

D.C. al Coda

out your love, it's a mel - o - dy played in a pen - ny ar - cade.

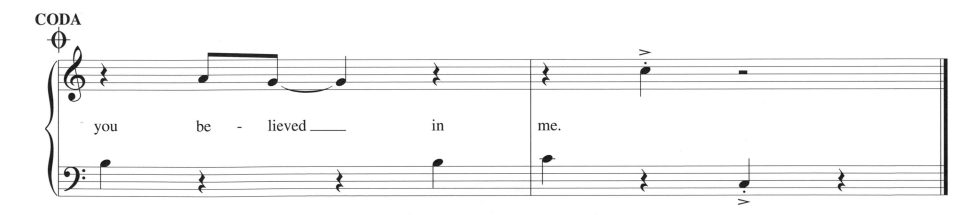

CODA

you be - lieved ___ in me.

Blue Skies
from BETSY

Words and Music by Irving Berlin
Arranged by Eric Baumgartner

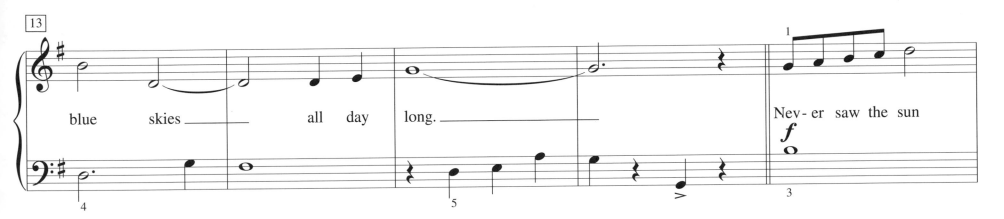

blue   skies ____ ____   all   day   long. ____ ____   Nev - er saw the sun

shin - ing so bright.   Nev - er saw things   go - ing so right.   No - tic - ing the days   hur - ry - ing   by;

CODA

when you're in   love,   my, how they   fly.

D.C. al Coda

on. ____ ____

Satin Doll
from SOPHISTICATED LADIES

Words by Johnny Mercer and Billy Strayhorn
Music by Duke Ellington
Arranged by Eric Baumgartner

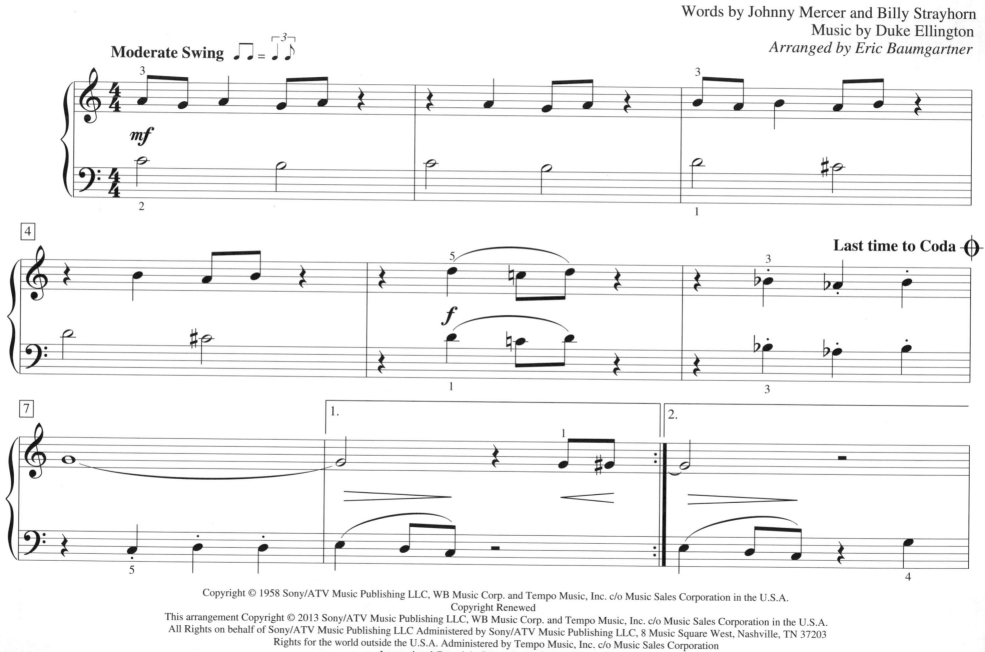

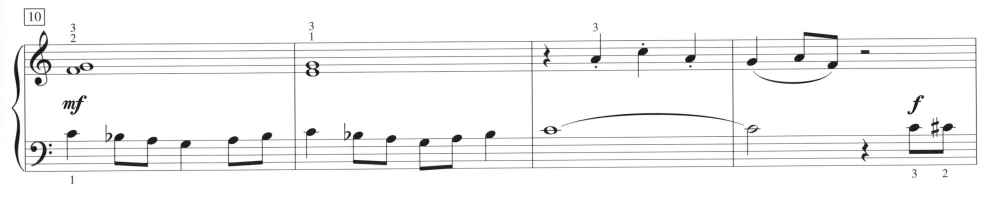

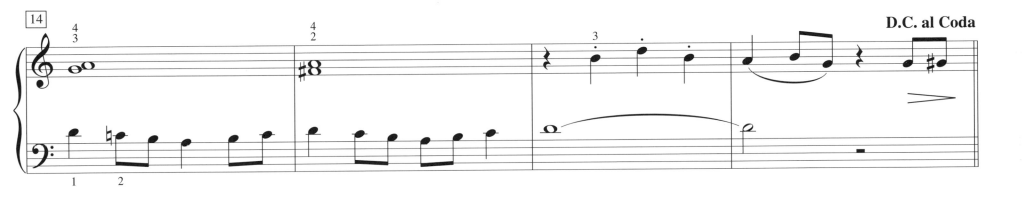

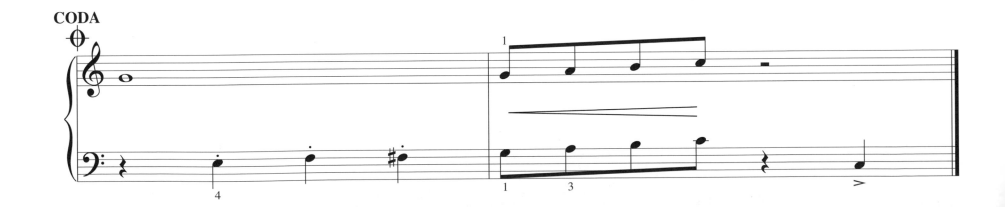

The Glory of Love

Words and Music by Billy Hill
Arranged by Eric Baumgartner

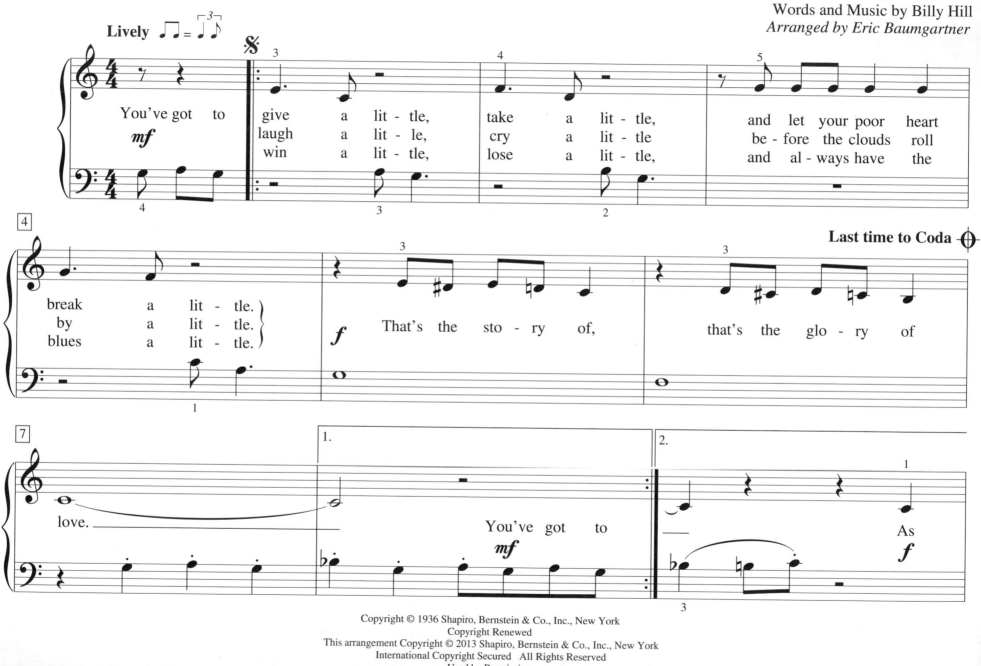

long   as there's   the   two   of   us,   we've   got   the   world   and   all   its

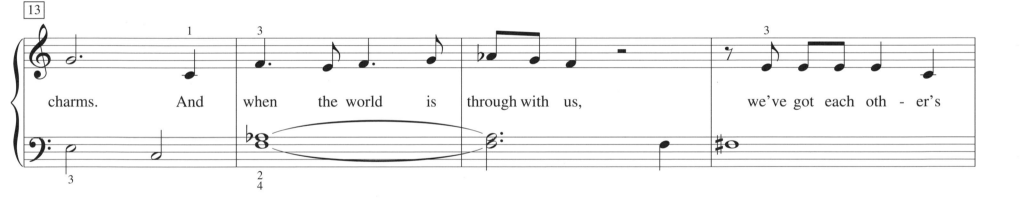

charms.   And   when   the   world   is   through with   us,   we've   got   each oth - er's

D.S. al Coda

CODA

arms.   You've   got   to

mf

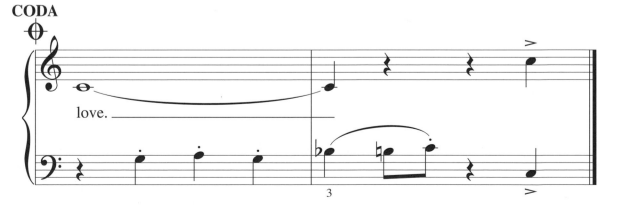

love.

Alexander's Ragtime Band

Words and Music by Irving Berlin
Arranged by Eric Baumgartner

Night Train

Words by Oscar Washington and Lewis C. Simpkins
Music by Jimmy Forrest
Arranged by Eric Baumgartner

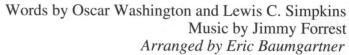